with a selection of photographs by
Jimmy Donald

Published by Newcastle upon Tyne
City Libraries and Arts

Front Cover
By the mid-nineteenth century Lord Armstrong had acquired the dene or valley of the Ouseburn. He fenced in the dene, planted it with trees and shrubs, built bridges across the stream and laid out walks along its banks. Having given the neighbouring Armstrong Park to the town in 1880 he next presented Jesmond Dene to the City in 1884 for use as a public park.

Acknowledgements

The photographs in this booklet were reproduced by kind permission of:

City of Newcastle upon Tyne City Libraries and Arts, City Engineers' Department (3, 8)

Newcastle upon Tyne City Libraries and Arts (the rest)

Published by Newcastle upon Tyne City Libraries and Arts, 1988, 1989.

ISBN 0902653 41 5

INTRODUCTION

early history of Jesmond is cure: some prehistoric remains e found in the nineteenth tury, but there are no known nan or Anglo-Saxon connections. name "Jesmond" probably ans "mouth of the Ouseburn", ough some people prefer the re fanciful "Jesus mound".

he twelfth century the manor of nond was given by Henry I to olas Grenville whose family built first manor house and at about the e time, St. Mary's Chapel. This ame a famous shrine, attracting rims from all over the country. Until 9, an eighteenth century Manor se (which replaced an earlier ding) stood on the original site at north end of Manor House Road.

l the middle of the nineteenth ury Jesmond was a mainly agricultural area, with several small coal mines. Thereafter it gradually, became a suburb of Newcastle, to which it was formerly added in 1835. Until the parish church was opened in 1861, Jesmond was part of St. Andrew, Newgate Street.

From about 1820 Jesmond became the home of Newcastle's shipbuilders, shipowners and other captains of industry, in their mansions such as Jesmond Dene House and the Towers (now La Sagesse Convent High School). Until 1916 Dr. Gibb of Blaydon Races fame had his villa at Sandyford Park, more recently known as Nazareth House. From 1820, also, date two of Jesmond' three villages: Brandling Village and Jesmond Vale, which were built for miners and industrial workers. The original Jesmond Village stood near the Manor House.

From the 1870s these villas and villages were progressively surrounded by suburban housing and from the 1880s Jesmond became the home of several well-known schools: the Church High School opened in 1885, followed by the Central High School, which moved to Eskdale Terrace in 1900. The Royal Grammar School moved to the area in 1906 and La Sagesse in 1912.

Osborne Road was laid out in the 1860s and 1870s; from 1880 it had a horse-drawn tram service as far as Mistletoe Road. This was replaced by electric trams in 1901, which later extended to North Jesmond Avenue. Trolleybuses served the area from 1938 until 1965. Jesmond had an electric train service from 1904, the forerunner of today's Metro.

JIMMY DONALD

1. Osborne Road at the end of the nineteenth century. The horse-drawn trams went up Osborne Road only as far as Mistletoe Road. They were replaced by electric trams in 1901. The Baptist Church founded in 1889 stood for almost a hundred years before being demolished in the 1970s to provide a site for sheltered housing. On the right the large house "Tyneholme", later to become a convent, was occupied by Thomas Pickering, a tea merchant.

The Manor of Jesmond was given to Nicholas Grenville in the twelfth century by Henry I. The original Manor House was rebuilt in the eighteenth century by William Coulson and stood until 1929 at the north end of Manor House Road.

3. St. Mary's Chapel was built in the mid-twelfth century by the Grenvilles. These lords of Jesmond may have brought back holy relics from the Crusades as the chapel became a place of pilgrimage. Lord Armstrong purchased the chapel and included it in his gift of Jesmond Dene to the City in 1884. These remains stand at the bottom of Reid Park Road.

STOTES HALL, NEWCASTLE·UPON·TYNE·

In 1658 Sir Richard Stote purchased a house with land attached and made it his residence. From that time the site of the house was always called Stotes Hall. As a young man the celebrated eighteenth century mathematician Dr. Charles Hutton kept a school in Stotes Hall. It was demolished in about 1953.

5. To the east of the Manor House stood the original village of Jesmond. Cottages adjoin the Apple Tree Inn and beyond them are the outbuildings of the Manor House. In the late nineteenth century many people travelled out from Newcastle to partake of the fine strawberries and cream served at this inn. The inn, cottages and Manor House have gone but the stone wall in the centre of the picture still stands at the bottom of Reid Park Road.

BRANDLING VILLAGE NEWCASTLE 1905

Brandling Village was built in 1820 on land belonging to Robert Warwick. It provided housing for workers employed in the Jesmond coal mines. The chimney of the Brandling Laundry where some of the village women worked can be seen in the background. It was a very close-knit community. Most of the village was demolished in the 1930s but some parts remain.

7. Jesmond vale village was built for workers employed in local pits and quarries. Two of the three village pubs shown, The Princess Royal and the Travellers Rest have now gone, but The Blue Bell (at left) still survives. The Ouseburn, which ran east of the village, overflowed its banks in 1903, when this picture was taken.

Newcastle General Cemetery was one of two private cemeteries laid out in Newcastle in the 1830s. It contains the graves of many prominent Newcastle people. John Dobson, who designed the lodges and gateway, is buried here.

9. Jesmond Towers was built in the early nineteenth century and was originally called West Jesmond House. About 1870 it was purchased by the shipbuilder Charles Mitchell, who enlarged and renamed it. His family lived there until the 1920s, since when it has been a school.

Charles Mitchell added a large picture gallery to Jesmond Towers to display his large collection of paintings and sculpture. When the contents of the house were auctioned in 1926, the paintings sold included works by T. M. Richardson, Ralph Hedley, Myles Birket Foster and Charles W. Mitchell, son of the shipbuilder.

11. St. George's Church, designed by T. R. Spence and consecrated in 1888, was built at the sole expense of the wealthy shipbuilder Charles Mitchell on the southern edge of his Jesmond Towers estate. The vicarage, at left, has been demolished.

Prominent shipbuilders lived in Jesmond in the late nineteenth century: Charles Mark Palmer,
Charles Mitchell and Henry F Swan, for example. This large semi-villa (of which there were a number
in Jesmond) was occupied by another shipbuilder, G. B. Hunter (of Swan, Hunter) from 1890 until
his death in 1937. It is still a family residence.

13. In 1884 the Church Schools Company purchased a small private school in Jesmond Road as the nucleus of a new school. Six years later they opened the Newcastle High School in this building in Tankerville Terrace. In 1925 it was renamed Newcastle upon Tyne Church High School.

The Northern Counties Orphanage, facing the Great North Road, was paid for by two prominent local families, the Abbots and the Philipsons. The building was sometimes referred to as the Abbot and Philipson Memorial Orphanage and continued as such until the outbreak of World War II. Subsequently the Princess Mary Maternity Hospital moved here from Jubilee Road.

15. Between 1860 and 1888 three new buildings were erected on Jesmond's western edge (the Moor Edge). These were the Northern Counties Institute for the Deaf and Dumb, the Northern Counties Orphanage and the Fleming Memorial Hospital for Sick Children. This hospital, the gift of Newcastle solicitor John Fleming, was opened in 1888 by Lord Armstrong and replaced the first children's hospital which had been opened in Hanover Square in 1863. The hospital site was formerly the Newcastle Cricket Club's ground.

This section of Osborne Road, looking north, was built in the 1880s. The traction poles carry the overhead wires for the new electric tram cars which were introduced in 1901. The street on the right is Holly Avenue.

CHURCH OF THE HOLY NAME, ST. GEORGES TERRACE, NEWCASTLE.

17. The Roman Catholic parish of the Holy Name was founded in 1901. A house in Manor House Road served as a chapel until 1903 when this temporary iron church was built in St. George's Terrace. After a permanent church was opened in Mitchell Avenue in 1929 the old iron church was used for social functions until the late 1930s when the site was sold for Jesmond swimming baths. Iron churches were very common in the late nineteenth century and could be purchased from a mail-order catalogue.

At the turn of the century much building took place between St. George's Terrace and the Town Moor; most of the new housing was two-flat dwellings. Much rented accommodation was available in Jesmond between the wars. Two delivery boys can be seen in this photograph of Tavistock Road.

19. These shops in St. George's Terrace date from the turn of the century when the Portland Estate, stretching from St. George's Terrace to Highbury was sold for building. Two handcarts used for making local deliveries stand in front of the shops. Present day shops here still form an important part of the Acorn Road shopping centre.

In the 1860s The Blyth and Tyne Railway line was laid through Jesmond. To regain passenger traffic which was being lost to the new tramway system the line was electrified in 1904. The picture shows one of the electric trains which ran between Newcastle and Tynemouth. The station-master's house on the left has been demolished and the station building is now a pub. A new Metro station has been opened north-west of the old station, whence the line goes underground to the City Centre.

21. This photograph of 1964 taken from near the Hancock Museum shows Jesmond Road at its junction with the Great North Road before the construction of the Central Motorway. The building on the left, behind the policeman was occupied by Chapman's furniture shop – Siesta House. The ambulance in the distance is passing Carlton House, once a fine private residence but then being used by the Municipal College of Commerce. The cheerful policeman on point duty will be remembered by many Newcastle motorists.